A History of Fashion and Costume

Volume 1
The Ancient World

Jane Bingham

☑® Facts On File, Inc.

The Ancient World

Produced for Facts On File by
Bailey Publishing Associates Ltd
11a Woodlands
Hove BN3 6TJ

Project Manager: Roberta Bailey
Editor: Alex Woolf
Text Designer: Simon Borrough
Artwork: Dave Burroughs, Peter Dennis,
   Tony Morris
Picture Research: Glass Onion Pictures

Printed and bound in Hong Kong

Facts On File, Inc.
132 West 31st Street
New York NY 10001

Facts On File books are available at special
discounts when purchased in bulk quantities for
businesses, associations, institutions, or sales
promotions. Please call our Special Sales
Department in New York at 212/967-8800 or
800/322-8755.

You can find Facts On File on the World Wide
Web at: http://www.factsonfile.com

Library of Congress Cataloging-in-Publication Data

Bingham, Jane.
A history of fashion and costume.
   Volume I, The ancient world/Jane
   Bingham.
     p. cm.
Includes bibliographical references and
   index.
   ISBN 0-8160-5944-6
   1. Clothing and dress—History—To
500.
   GT530.B56 2005
   391/.009/01—dc 22   2004060881

The publishers would like to thank the
following for permission to use their
pictures:

Art Archive: 7, 8, 9, 10, 11, 14. 15
(both), 16, 19, 21, 22, 25 (bottom), 26,
27, 28, 30, 32, 33, 34, 35, 36, 37, 39, 40,
41, 43, 45, 47, 48 (top), 49, 51, 53 (top),
54 (both), 55, 56, 57, 58, 59
Werner Forman Archive: 12, 13, 25
(top), 38, 48 (bottom), 53 (bottom)

Contents

Introduction

This volume traces the history of costume from the last Ice Age, when people first started wearing clothes, to the collapse of the Roman Empire in the late fifth century CE. Divided into chapters according to region, it outlines the early history of costume from prehistoric times to the emergence of the first cities, and surveys the succession of civilizations that grew up in the Middle East. Individual chapters are devoted to ancient Egypt, Greece, and Rome, but the book also focuses on the cultures of India, eastern Asia, and the Pacific region. The final chapter covers the rich civilizations of the Americas.

The history of costume is a vast subject, and the aim of this volume is simply to highlight major trends and to provide interesting examples. Knowledge of ancient costume depends on surviving evidence (such as paintings and items of jewelry), and while it is sometimes possible to build up a detailed portrait of a culture, the picture is far from complete for many civilizations.

Although the cultures described in this book are extremely varied, they all have some factors in common. Most early civilizations had a strong ruler, who dressed in a dramatic way to show off his riches and power. Warriors needed weapons and armor to help them defend their kingdoms. People wore special costumes to worship their gods, and both men and women liked to adorn themselves with jewelry and ornaments. Once a society was reasonably settled, traders exchanged goods for precious items that were used to create fine jewelry and costumes.

Chapter 1: Early People

Prehistoric People

The hunters of the last Ice Age, who lived around 100,000 years ago, were probably the first people to wear clothes. However, there is no proof of when clothing first developed, since the materials used to make clothing decay easily and rapidly, and the earliest examples of clothing did not survive. Recent DNA evidence indicates that some time between 30,000 and 114,000 years ago, head lice, which typically infest human hair, evolved a new sub-species, body lice, which commonly infest human clothing.

Prehistoric people wore simple clothes made from animal skins, and added jewelry and ornaments made from shells, bones and feathers.

Making Clothes

The first clothes were probably simple tunics, trousers, string skirts, belts, and cloaks. These were sometimes made from fur, although this could be very bulky. More often the fur was removed from the animal hide. However, people did wear fur boots, tied onto their feet and legs with leather laces.

To make clothing, animal hides were first pegged out on the ground and scraped clean, using a sharpened animal bone or sharp-edged stone. Then they were washed and stretched out taut to stop them from shrinking as they dried. Once the hides had been thoroughly stretched, the leather was softened before being cut into suitable pieces for clothing. Then a sharp, pointed stone was used to punch a line of holes along the edges of the leather pieces. The holes made it easier to pass a bone needle through the hide and sew the pieces together, using sinew.

Early Decorations

Evidence survives from around 30,000 years ago of hunters decorating their clothes. The mammoth hunters of the Russian plains sewed seashells and feathers onto their tunics. They also made strings of beads from shells and animal teeth, and used ivory from mammoth tusks to make simple bracelets. Archaeologists believe that the mammoth hunters wore these decorations for religious ceremonies and dances.

Cave Paintings

Around 35,000 years ago, people began painting pictures on the walls of caves. Some of these early cave paintings depict semi-human creatures, and experts believe that these figures were probably priests dressed as animals. The painted, dancing figures wear deer antlers attached to their heads, and long wolves' tails. They also appear to be wearing cloaks made from feathers.

Body Paints

There is evidence that the early cave painters painted their bodies as well as their caves. Traces of red ocher pigment have been discovered on bodies in graves, suggesting that people decorated the bodies of the dead before they were buried. It is probable that people also used pigments to paint patterns on their own bodies, just as people have done for millions of years in Africa and Australia. Specialized tools for permanent tattooing dating from around 38,000 years ago have been discovered in Europe.

Shells were one of the first materials to be made into jewelry. These very early carved and painted ornaments reflect an ancient tradition of jewelry making.

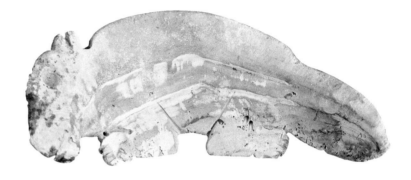

Where's the Evidence?

Archaeologists draw on a range of different sources to build up a picture of the sort of clothes that very early people wore. Scraps of leather clothing have been found in graves, while shells and teeth pierced with holes indicate that these objects once formed necklaces. To help them reconstruct the practices of ancient people, archaeologists also study traditional groups, such as the aboriginals of Australia and the Inuit of Alaska, who have followed the same basic way of life for thousands of years.

First Civilizations

Even in the earliest civilizations, color and pattern were very important. This painted plaque from the twelfth century BCE shows a woman from Nubia (in North Africa) and a man from Syria, both dressed in colorful costumes.

Dyes from Nature

Early people colored their clothes with dyes made from earth, flowers, and bark, and in some parts of the world people still use these natural dyes. A type of clay called ocher produces warm reds, oranges, and yellows. The indigo plant makes a deep blue, while the madder root gives a rich scarlet. Some lichens produce a green color, while the bark and husks of walnut dye cloth a deep brown.

Ancient Sumerians

One of the earliest civilizations in the Middle East was the kingdom of Sumer, which lay between the Tigris and Euphrates rivers in present-day Iraq. The civilization began around 3500 BCE with a collection of villages, and by 3000 BCE it contained several large city-states, each ruled by a warlike king with his own army.

The ancient Sumerians learned how to make objects from copper, silver, and gold by heating metal ore and pouring it into molds. Their metalworkers became very skilled, producing engraved necklaces, daggers, and helmets. The Sumerians made another important discovery: by combining copper and tin, they created bronze, a very strong alloy that could be used to make axes, spears, and more robust helmets.

The ancient Sumerians wore colorful robes with scalloped hems. Rulers had tall headdresses, while dancers and musicians wore sleeveless robes with multi-tiered skirts. Soldiers wore knee-length tunics with scalloped hems and long cloaks fastened at the neck. They fought with long spears and wore pointed helmets. The production of cloth for export was very important to the economy and culture of ancient Sumeria. They even had a goddess of weaving and clothing, named Uttu.

Sumerian men paid a lot of attention to their hair. A golden helmet found in a royal tomb in the ancient city of Ur is engraved with hair and ears, revealing that warriors wore their hair in an elaborate style: hanging down in curls around the ears, braided at the front, and fastened in a knot at the back of the head. A similar braided hairstyle is shown in a bronze head of King Sargon (reigned c. 2334–c. 2284 BCE), who ruled the land of Akkad, just to the north of Sumer. In addition to his elaborate hairstyle, the king also sported a splendid curled beard, carefully trimmed to fall in two tiers.

A bronze head of King Sargon of Akkad, showing the elaborate hairstyle and carefully trimmed beard favored by the nobles of Sumer.

Chapter 2: Ancient Egypt

Clothing and Jewelry

Around 5000 BCE farming villages began to grow up around the Nile River in northern Africa. Gradually, from around 3100 BCE, the villages of the Nile joined together to form a great kingdom, ruled by powerful pharaohs. The Egyptian civilization flourished for three thousand years. Historians divide it into three main periods, or kingdoms: the Old, the Middle, and the New Kingdom.

An Egyptian pharaoh from the New Kingdom being anointed with oil by his queen. Both figures wear pleated robes of fine royal linen, and have ornate collars and elaborate crowns.

Egyptian farmers, like the figures shown here, wore short kilts made from coarse linen.

Using Linen

In the hot and sunny climate of North Africa, which in ancient times was also very humid, the ancient Egyptians did not need to wear heavy clothes. Clothing was made from linen, which was cool and easy to wear. Linen thread was made from the beaten stalks of the flax plant and woven on looms into cloth. Ordinary people wore simple clothes made from coarse, unbleached linen, while nobles' clothes were made from a fine, white, semi-transparent cloth known as royal linen.

Clothing Styles

For thousands of years the basic style of Egyptian clothes remained unchanged. Women wore a simple, tight-fitting, ankle-length dress with two shoulder straps, while men wore a kilt, made from a piece of linen wrapped around the waist and tucked in. Kilts could be either knee- or ankle-length. In winter, men and women wore cloaks made from thick linen.

Tunics and kilts were usually kept plain. Although their clothes could be decorated with beads and feathers, the Egyptian people relied on their jewelry, makeup, and hairstyles to create a dramatic effect.

During the time of the New Kingdom, a more elaborate style of dress developed in Egypt. Tunics and cloaks made of very fine, pleated cloth became fashionable for men and women. Over their basic tunic women began to wear a pleated garment that sometimes had a brightly colored fringe and small ornaments hanging from it. Some men wore a long, almost transparent kilt over their short tunic.

Jewelry

No Ancient Egyptian costume was complete without a selection of jewelry. Even poorer people wore necklaces, bracelets, and earrings. Poor people's jewelry was made from cheaper substances such as copper and faience (a colored, glazed pottery), while the rich wore

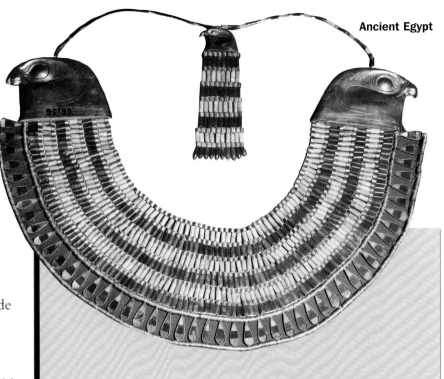

This fine collar belonged to an Egyptian princess. It is decorated with golden hawks' heads and inlaid with colored glass and semiprecious stones.

Colorful Collars

One of the most impressive items of Egyptian jewelry was the broad, decorative collar. These collars were worn by both women and men of all classes. The collars consisted of a series of strings threaded with beads and ornaments, but also with flowers, berries, and leaves. Some of the collars found in the pharaoh Tutankhamun's tomb included olive leaves and cornflowers.

spectacular pieces made from gold and silver and often set with semiprecious stones and glass.

Footwear

People in ancient Egypt went barefoot most of the time, but sometimes they wore sandals. Rich people's sandals were made from decorated leather, and one pair of golden sandals has been discovered in a pharaoh's tomb. Poor people's sandals were made from papyrus (a type of reed) or from woven grass.

Egyptian Beauty Care

In this painted banquet scene, four young women wear braided wigs decorated with lotus flower blossoms. The artist has also shown cones of fat resting on top of the women's heads (see Cool Cones).

Looking good was very important to the ancient Egyptians. They worked hard to keep themselves clean and sweet-smelling, and both men and women used cosmetics, which they kept in elegant pots. The Egyptians also paid a lot of attention to their hair, and some rich people shaved their heads and wore elaborate wigs.

Hair and Wigs

Most Egyptian men were clean-shaven and kept their hair fairly short, although some noblemen had longer hair. In the early periods, women usually had a chin-length bob, but by the time of the New Kingdom noblewomen wore their hair long. These long tresses were sometimes worn loose and sometimes curled and braided. Noblewomen liked to decorate their hair with flowers, beads, and ribbons.

Pharaohs and nobles often shaved their heads and wore elaborate wigs. Less wealthy people also wore wigs, but only for special occasions. Egyptian wigs could be amazingly elaborate, with lots of braids and curls. Some wigs had ornaments hung over them, or were decorated with beads and jewels. The best wigs were made from real hair, but there were also cheaper ones made from black wool.

Cool Cones

Paintings of ancient Egyptian banquets show the guests with rounded cones on their heads. It is believed that these were cones of perfumed fat that gradually melted during the course of the meal, keeping the guests cool and also ensuring that they smelled sweet. However, some experts believe that the cones were drawn by artists to indicate that the person was wearing a scented wig.

Children had their hair shaved off or cut very short, except for one section that formed a kind of ponytail on one side. This s-shaped lock was called the "side-lock of youth." Sometimes children wore a fish amulet in their hair, perhaps to protect them from drowning in the Nile.

Cosmetics

Egyptian cosmetics were made from finely ground minerals mixed with oils. Green and black eyeliners were made from malachite (copper ore) and galena (a type of lead), while red ocher was used for lipstick and blush. The Egyptians took a lot of care over making up their eyes; they outlined them with heavy lines, which drew attention to the beauty of the eyes and also helped to shield them from the glare of the sun. Green eyeliner was used in the early period, but later black became very popular. Red-brown henna, made from the leaves of the henna tree, was used to paint nails and possibly hands and feet, and henna was also used to dye hair and wigs.

Cosmetics were prepared and stored in jars and bowls, and sometimes in hollow reeds. Makeup was applied with the fingers or with a special wooden applicator. To help them apply their makeup, the rich used mirrors made from highly polished metal. Poor people had to manage by observing their reflections in water!

Smelling Sweet

In the hot climate of Egypt it was very important to keep clean. Most people washed in the river or used a basin and jug of water. Instead of soap they used a cleansing cream made from oil, lime, and perfume. They also rubbed scented oils into their skin to stop it from drying out in the sun. Perfumes were made from flowers, seeds, and fruits soaked in oils and animal fats.

This decorated makeup box belonged to the wife of an important architect. The glass and ceramic jars would have held perfumes, oils and cosmetics.

Pharaohs, Queens, and Priests

Religion was central to ancient Egyptian society. The Egyptians believed that their land had originally been ruled by gods, whose power had passed directly to the pharaohs. So pharaohs and their families were treated like gods and wore highly elaborate ceremonial costumes.

Pharaohs

One of the most important elements of the pharaoh's dress was his crown or headdress. Early kings often wore a red-and-white crown symbolizing the two parts of their kingdom: red for lower Egypt and white for upper Egypt. Rulers of the New Kingdom wore a bright blue crown like a battle helmet, reflecting their important role as a warrior. Later rulers, such as Tutankhamun, often wore a long, striped headdress called a *menes*. The *menes* was usually decorated with the heads of the pharaoh's twin protectors: the vulture and the cobra.

In paintings and carvings, pharaohs are often shown holding the symbols of their office: the royal crook and flail. The crook symbolized the pharaoh's protection of his people, while the flail stood for the punishment of his enemies.

Queens

The pharaoh had many queens, but the chief queen was usually his sister or half-sister. She was believed to be a goddess and was dressed in astonishing splendor. Paintings and carvings show Egyptian queens wearing tall, jeweled headdresses, golden collars, armlets, and finger rings.

Priests

Priests wore only the finest, pure white linen. They had to purify themselves by bathing in a sacred lake at least twice a day. They also had to shave their whole bodies, including their hair and eyebrows. Most of the time the priests dressed simply to carry out their duties in the temples, but sometimes they wore special costumes and headdresses. In the final stages of the embalming ceremony

This solid gold burial mask comes from the tomb of the Pharaoh Tutankhamun (1332-1322 BCE). It shows the young king wearing the striped menes, with its twin symbols of the vulture and the cobra, and carrying his royal crook and flail.

False Beard

Most Egyptian men were clean-shaven, but pharaohs wore a long beard that grew from the base of their chin, as a sign of their royal status. At one point in Egyptian history, between 1473 and 1458 BCE, a woman ruled as the pharaoh. Carvings show that Queen Hatshepsut was properly crowned as pharaoh and wore the full royal regalia, including a false beard!

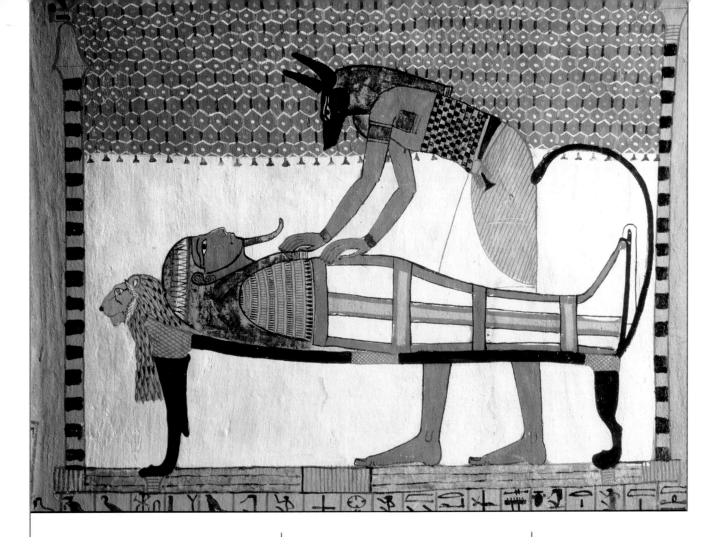

(when a dead body was being prepared to be a mummy), the chief priest wore a jackal mask. This dramatic, painted mask, which covered his whole head and shoulders, represented the god Anubis.

Amulets

Many items of jewelry worn by ordinary Egyptians featured good-luck charms, known as amulets. The amulets depicted religious symbols such as the ankh (a cross with a loop at the top) representing eternal life, or the *udjat* eye (the eye of the god Horus) symbolizing healing and good health. Sometimes these charms took the form of ornaments or brooches. In other cases, a sacred symbol was

painted or carved into a piece of jewelry. Some necklaces and earrings featured charms to ward off snake bites!

A chief priest, wearing his ceremonial mask, tends the body of a dead pharaoh. The mask represents Anubis, the jackal god. According to ancient Egyptian belief, he led the dead to judgment.

The Pharaoh Akhenaten and his wife, Queen Nefertiti, who reigned in the 1350s BCE, dressed in semi-transparent robes and simple crowns. For grand ceremonial occasions, Egyptian rulers wore more elaborate costumes.

Chapter 3: Peoples of Western Asia

Around 2000 BCE the ancient civilization of Sumer (see page 9) collapsed. This was the start of a turbulent period in the Middle East, as many different peoples battled for control of the fertile lands around the Persian Gulf and the eastern Mediterranean Sea. Over the next 1,500 years, a series of powerful kingdoms rose and fell. Many of these civilizations were very warlike, some were great traders, and some produced fine buildings and works of art.

Hittite warriors wore leather tunics covered with iron plates. To protect their heads they had iron helmets with a distinctive crest, which was probably made from horsehair.

Hittites, Canaanites, and Sea Peoples

Around 2000 BCE the Hittite people settled in Anatolia (modern-day Turkey), and within four hundred years they had conquered an empire that stretched as far south as present-day Syria. For more than two centuries they were one of Egypt's most dangerous enemies.

The Hittites were tough warriors who developed a new and effective battle dress. When they rode into battle in their war chariots, they dressed in leather tunics covered with metal plates, giving them excellent protection against enemy spears and arrows. Hittite warriors carried long wooden spears tipped with iron, which were much stronger than the bronze weapons of their opponents. They wore iron helmets with flaps to protect their neck, and carried large wicker shields.

Cloth from Canaan

To the south of the Hittite empire lay the more peaceful land of Canaan. Most of the Canaanites were farmers and merchants, and Canaan had several thriving ports on the Mediterranean coast. Weavers in Canaan produced a colorful, patterned cloth that was sold by merchants to people all around the Mediterranean. Wool and linen were dyed in a range of brilliant colors, including scarlet, green, blue, and gold, and bold patterns and borders were woven into the cloth. The people of Canaan made their colorful cloth into striking clothes. Some wore several layers of different patterns, while others preferred a simple, long, white tunic, edged with a dramatic band of color.

Sea Peoples

Eventually, the Hittite empire was destroyed by an army of Sea Peoples (also sometimes called Philistines), who originally came from Greece. The Sea Peoples wore short, colorful tunics decorated with bold, contrasting bands of color. They fought with iron-tipped spears and swords, and protected themselves with round, wooden shields. One of their tribes, called the Sherden, wore distinctive battle helmets, crowned by two small horns. The horns may have had a religious significance or they may have simply been intended to make the warriors appear more frightening. The warrior Goliath, whose fight against David is recorded in the Bible, was a member of the Sea Peoples.

Two armed warriors from the army of the Sea Peoples. The soldier on the left wears the distinctive horned helmet of the Sherden tribe.

Hebrews

The story of the Hebrews is told in the Old Testament of the Bible. They were a wandering desert people who gained control of some land in Canaan between 1200 and 1050 BCE. Around 1000 BCE the Hebrew king David (reigned c. 1005–c. 965 BCE) established the kingdom of Israel with its capital city in Jerusalem. The kingdom split in two in about 931, and the northern kingdom, called Israel, was conquered by the Assyrians (see pages 22–3) around 722. The southern kingdom, Judah, was attacked by the Babylonians (see page 24) in 597, and ten years later the Babylonians destroyed Jerusalem. The Hebrews, who came to be known as Jews, were taken into captivity.

A Hebrew priest wearing the "white garments"—a turban, tunic, breeches and belt all made from pure white linen. These garments were worn as a sign of humility before God.

Most Hebrews dressed very simply in tunics or long dresses. To keep off the glare of the sun, people often wore a cloth over their head, which was fixed in place with a narrow headband. Hebrew kings, however, wore rich robes, adorned with precious stones, while the most magnificent costume of all was worn by the high priest.

Ceremonial Garments

Around 950 BCE King David's son Solomon (reigned c. 965–c. 931 BCE) built a spectacular temple in Jerusalem to house his people's most precious treasure, the Ark of the Covenant. The high priest in charge of the temple wore a special set of ceremonial clothes known as the golden garments. According to Jewish belief, God gave the prophet Moses detailed instructions for the making of these sacred garments, and these instructions are all recorded in the Book of Exodus in the Old Testament.

The golden garments consisted of eight separate items: a tunic, a belt, a turban, a pair of linen breeches, a breastplate, an ephod (a type of apron), a robe, and a golden head plate. Over the white tunic and pants, the high priest wore a sky-blue robe, hemmed with decorative pomegranates and bells which tinkled as he moved. On top of the tunic was the ephod, with two sardonyx stones on its shoulder-straps, and a breastplate, set with twelve precious stones, representing the twelve tribes of Israel. Finally, the turban was placed on the high priest's head, and the golden head plate fixed in place with its inscription, "Holy to the Lord."

The high priest wore his golden garments every day of the year except on the Day of Atonement, the Hebrews' most holy day. On this day, the high priest showed his humility before God by wearing the white garments: a turban, tunic, breeches, and belt, all made from pure white linen. Other priests wore the white garments all through the year.

Special Materials

The Book of Exodus lists five different materials to be used in the making of the golden garments: gold, sky-blue wool, dark red wool, crimson wool, and "twisted linen." Many years of research have gone into discovering exactly which materials were used. The evidence suggests that gold leaf was beaten into thin sheets, and then cut into fine threads; the sky-blue dye for the wool came from a shellfish known as chilazon; the dark red color was derived from a type of snail; and the crimson color was produced by the cochineal insect. To weave the tunic, turban, and breeches, a thick linen thread was used, made from six twisted strands.

This 13th century fresco shows Abraham being blessed by a High Priest. While Abraham is shown in the costume of a medieval knight, the High Priest wears his ceremonial robes.

Joseph's Coat

In the Old Testament Book of Genesis, Joseph, the youngest son of Jacob, is described as having a glorious "coat of many colors." Nobody knows what this coat would have looked like, but it may have featured colored wool dyed sky blue and crimson, as well as the more usual greens, yellows, and browns produced by earth and plants.

Phoenicians

The Phoenicians were a seafaring people descended from the Canaanites (see page 16). From around 1200 BCE they lived along the eastern coast of the Mediterranean Sea, setting up great trading ports. For two thousand years the Phoenicians were the most successful traders in the region. As well as their kingdom in the Middle East, they also had colonies along the coasts of Africa and Spain, and in Cyprus, Sicily, and Malta.

Purple People

The word Phoenician is Greek for "purple men," a name the

Phoenician men wore long tunics with multi-tiered, fringed skirts.

Phoenicians acquired because of their famous purple dye. Made from the murex shellfish, the dye colored cloth a rich, deep purple. Purple cloth from Phoenicia was sold all over the Mediterranean and the Middle East, but it was so expensive that it was usually only worn by royalty.

Stylish Dressers

Phoenician men were stylish dressers, who liked to show off their wealth by wearing colorful clothes. While the ordinary workers wore simple loincloths, rulers and merchants often wore long tunics, with multi-tiered skirts. Each tier was bordered by a fringe. Many Phoenician men wore a conical cap, but those who went bareheaded paid a lot of attention to their hair and beard, which were both carefully curled.

Wealthy men wore jewelry, including broad neck collars similar to those worn by the ancient Egyptians, and simple armlets consisting of a twist of metal wound several times around the upper arm. Merchants and rulers wore finger rings set with semiprecious stones that were engraved with a design, and these rings could be stamped into wax and used as a personal seal.

Gorgeous Jewels

Phoenician women were usually modestly dressed, draping their bodies in folds of cloth. Their hair was often covered by a cap or hood, but sometimes it was simply encircled by a band, below which it rippled freely over their shoulders.

Jewelry was very popular with Phoenician women, who wore a variety of pendants, armlets, bracelets, earrings, finger rings, and brooches. Another type of ornament was the flat, patterned plaque, usually made from glass, with holes in the edges, which was apparently sewn onto clothes.

Often, Phoenician ladies wore three or four necklaces at a time, one above the other—a string of small pearls at the top, then some larger beads, and finally a couple of rows of necklaces with hanging ornaments (similar to a present-day charm bracelet). Some surviving necklaces have up to sixty ornaments made from gold, glass, and precious stones. The ornaments came in an astonishing variety of shapes, including acorns, pomegranates, lotus flowers, miniature vases and cones, and the heads of humans and animals.

A Phoenician glass bead, greatly magnified. Beads like this were traded all around the Mediterranean area.

Phoenician women were famous for their splendid jewelry.

Glass Beads

The Phoenicians were probably the earliest people to discover how to blow glass, and they made a range of beautiful colored beads. Many surviving Phoenician beads are long and oval in shape and blue-green in color. Others are a deep olive green. As well as making beads from solid glass, the Phoenicians also created tiny sculptures in colored glass. Some of these beads, showing human heads, contain up to five different colors of glass, and are impressively detailed, with tiny coils of glass for hair and beards.

Assyrians

An Assyrian king and queen relaxing in their garden. Both wear golden jewelry and colorful robes covered with embroidered patterns.

The Assyrian people were farmers who came from an area close to the Tigris River in present-day Iraq. From around 1350 BCE they began to conquer new land. Over the next seven hundred years, they built up a large empire which stretched from the Persian Gulf to the eastern Mediterranean, and even reached as far west as Egypt. The Assyrian kings were great war leaders, but they also loved to relax in their beautiful palaces and gardens.

Battle Dress

The Assyrians were expert warriors, who fought with bows and arrows, spears and swords, and long leather

This carved relief from the ancient city of Nineveh shows two armed warriors—one with a bow and arrows and the other carrying a wooden shield shaped like a shallow cone.

Splendid Beards

Assyrian hair and beards were very well tended. A statue of King Ashurnasirpal II (reigned 668–c. 627 BCE) shows his carefully curled, shoulder-length hair and a splendid moustache and beard. The beard is carefully trimmed into a neat rectangle and appears to have bands of horizontal decoration. Other Assyrian statues also feature beards with decorated horizontal bands, and it is possible that the Assyrians' beards were bound or interwoven with embroidered cloth.

slings. Soldiers wore short, belted tunics, leggings, and high leather boots. Some carried round wooden shields into battle and some were protected by an extra leather tunic covered with many small iron plates. Most warriors wore pointed iron helmets with flaps to cover their ears, and some of their helmets were topped with a plume of feathers. Kings rode into battle in a royal war chariot, wearing long robes and a fez-shaped golden helmet.

Horses played an important part in Assyrian warfare and they were also dressed for battle. They wore golden collars with a bunch of scarlet feathers hanging down at the front. The royal horses also had a crown of feathers on their heads.

Palace Life

Assyrian men at court usually wore a close-fitting, short-sleeved tunic, edged with golden fringes. Tunics were usually worn long, but some stopped at the knees and sometimes a fringed shawl was also worn. Except in the earliest examples, Assyrian costumes were lavishly decorated, and the robes of the king were covered with embroidery. The king wore a golden, fez-shaped crown and wherever he went in his palace, a servant accompanied him, holding a fringed canopy, like a parasol over his head.

The Assyrians were skilled workers in gold, and both men and women wore golden necklaces, bracelets, and earrings. Assyrian noblewomen dressed in a similar way to men, in fringed and embroidered robes and shawls, which covered them from neck to ankle. Both women and men at court wore simple leather sandals on their feet.

Fabrics, Colors, and Patterns

The most common material for clothing was wool, although linen was sometimes used for better-quality garments. Clothes were dyed in a range of colors: pale and deep indigo blue, scarlet, yellow ocher, dull olive green, and purple. All of these colors were also used to dye embroidery wool. Patterns embroidered on Assyrian clothes featured repeated geometric shapes, and often included sacred rosettes and palm trees.

Babylonians

Babylon had a period of greatness during the eighteenth century BCE, when it was ruled by King Hamurabai. However, after 1750, the city gradually declined, and was finally conquered by the Assyrians in 689 BCE. Then, around 620 BCE, the Babylonians began to fight back. By the time King Nebuchadnezzar II came to the throne in 605 BCE, Babylon had taken control of the Assyrian Empire. The Babylonians ruled their empire for the next sixty years, before being conquered by the Persians.

Dress in Babylon

One of King Nebuchadnezzar's greatest achievements was the rebuilding of Babylon. During his reign it became one of the richest cities in the world, full of temples and palaces and home to the famous hanging gardens.

Inside the splendid city of Babylon, the wealthy lived a life of comfort and ceremony. Men and women wore a loose, flowing tunic, with wide half-sleeves, caught in at the waist by a broad, decorative belt. Men carried tall, ornamental staffs and wore a fez-like headdress. Tunics were made from dyed linen, and a second, woolen tunic was sometimes also worn when the weather became cooler. Servants in Babylon wore simple, short, undyed tunics, belted at the waist. One of their tasks was to walk in front of their wealthy masters with a large whisk, driving away the flies!

The people of Babylon were skilled workers in silver and gold, and both men and women loved to wear golden jewelry. A surviving statue of the goddess Ishtar shows her wearing a necklace made from concentric golden rings and two outsize golden earrings—one resembling a bunch of grapes and the other, a shell.

Two Babylonian servants accompany their richly dressed master.

Persians

The land of Persia (present-day Iran) was originally ruled by two separate tribes: the Persians in the south, and the Medes in the north. Then, in 550 BCE, the Persians took over the Medes' land and began to conquer all of the surrounding lands. By the year 500, the Persians ruled the largest empire the world had ever seen. The mighty Persian Empire lasted for two hundred years until it was finally defeated by Alexander the Great.

The Persians and Medes wore very distinctive headdresses. While the Persians had tall, fluted hats, the Medes wore a plain, rounded bonnet, with a tail hanging down at the back. Persian men tended to wear their beards long, and often wore golden hoops in their ears.

Soldiers and Satraps

A tiled frieze survives showing Persian soldiers in ceremonial dress. The soldiers wear long, patterned robes, with wide, pleated sleeves. Each soldier wears a wide, golden band encircling his forehead, and carries a tall spear and a bow slung over his shoulder. Attached to each soldier's back is a deep pouch for carrying arrows.

At court, the Persians wore long, flowing robes with pleated sleeves, but the local rulers, known as satraps,

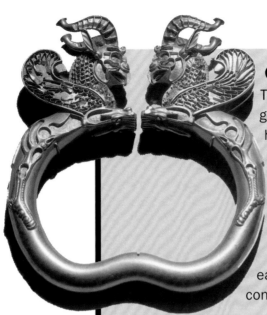

Golden Armlet

The Persians made exquisite golden jewelry. A solid gold armlet has been discovered at Oxus (in present-day Turkmenistan) in a hoard of treasure that probably belonged to a Persian king. The armlet is covered with elaborate carvings and shows two mythical, birdlike creatures, with beaks, ears, horns, and wings, each confronting the other fiercely.

dressed far more simply in short, woolen tunics and long pants. The Persians were great horsemen, and pants were very practical for long horse rides across the plains.

Persian guards with spears and shields, carved on a staircase in the royal palace at Persepolis.

Scythians

One group of people who the Persians never succeeded in conquering were the warlike Scythians. They lived as nomads on the windswept plains north of the Black Sea, in an area that is now Russia. The Scythians spent much of their lives on horseback, herding sheep and cattle. They set up their tents wherever they could find good pasture, and fought fiercely to defend their lands.

Animal Art

Because of their nomadic lifestyle, the Scythians created an art that was easily portable, making intricate golden jewelry and weapons, decorative tent hangings, and carved wooden bowls. They also decorated their clothes and made elaborate trappings for their horses. All these objects were ornamented with swirling animal motifs featuring horses, stags, eagles, bears, snakes, and rabbits.

Scythian warriors carry their dead leader's armlets and robes in a solemn funeral procession. They are wearing distinctive pointed felt caps.

Herders and Warriors

Scythian herders and warriors needed warm clothes that were easy to ride in. They wore leather, fur-lined boots, thick woolen pants, and tunics which wrapped across their bodies and were fastened by a belt. On their heads they wore a thick pointed cap which covered their ears.

When they rode into battle, Scythian warriors wore a protective armor of overlapping metal plates, which covered their upper body and sometimes their legs. Helmets were also made from metal plates. The warriors fought with long-bladed battleaxes and bows and arrows, and they often engraved their arrow cases with animal designs.

Scythian women spent less time on horseback, but they also dressed warmly in long woolen dresses, topped by a belted coat. They wore tall headdresses swathed in scarves.

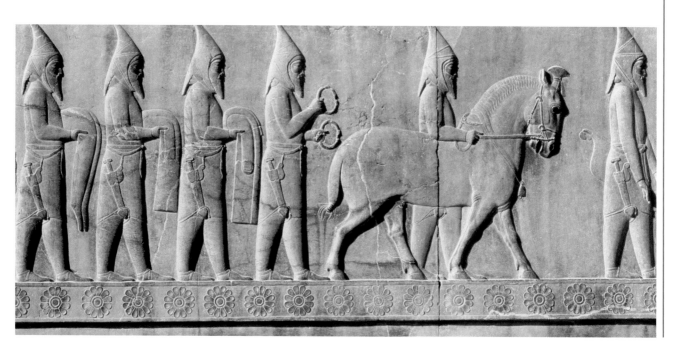

Splendid Decorations

The Scythians' clothes were made from leather and wool and covered in decoration. Women embroidered elaborate animal patterns in colored wool and also stitched felt appliqué pieces onto dresses, tunics, and coats. Felt was made by pressing and rolling wool and hair until it formed a thick, matted substance which was dyed vivid colors. The Scythians created dramatic appliqué designs on their wall hangings, horse trappings, and clothes, using shapes made from colored felt.

In addition to these decorations, the Scythians also sewed small, golden plaques onto their clothes. These plaques were engraved with animal motifs and must have sparkled dramatically in the sun, especially when worn in combination with elaborate golden belts, necklaces, bracelets, and earrings.

Animal Tattoos

The graves of several Scythian chiefs were excavated in Siberia. The bodies have stayed frozen in the icy ground for thousands of years and still display tattoos on their skin. The tattoos are remarkably elaborate and show swirling designs of interlocked creatures that appear to be a combination of horses, eagles, and stags.

Ceremonial Dress

The Scythians kept their best clothes for special ceremonies, such as the burial of a chief. When a chief was buried, his body was dressed in the most splendid finery and laid on a chariot, which was pulled by a pair of horses in ceremonial dress. The horses were draped in appliquéd hangings and wore golden harnesses and tall, tasseled headdresses. Men in the funeral procession shaved their heads, and some even cut off an ear to show their grief.

The Scythians were expert goldsmiths. This exquisite golden comb, found in a chief's tomb, shows Scythian warriors in battle.

Chapter 4: Civilizations of Ancient Greece

Minoans

The first great civilization in Europe grew up on the Greek island of Crete. The Minoan civilization started slowly, and developed over several thousand years, but by 2000 BCE there were a number of palaces on the island, each ruled by a king. In the warm, sunny Mediterranean climate, agriculture thrived. The Minoans farmed, fished, made pottery, and worked gold.

This fresco from the Minoan palace at Knossos shows a procession of priestesses, all wearing full-skirted dresses with low-cut bodices.

Minotaur Mask?

According to Greek legend, the first king of Crete kept a beast called a 'minotaur' in a huge maze under his palace. This creature had a bull's head and a man's body. Some scholars believe that this legend had its origin in a ceremony performed at the palace, in which the king wore a mask of a bull's head.

Minoan Dress

Colorful paintings on the walls of the Minoan palaces reveal the sort of clothes that people wore on the island. Minoan men usually wore a simple loincloth or a short kilt made from wool or linen. The kilts dipped down to form a point at the front, and they were often decorated with geometric patterns and a patterned border. Minoan men were usually clean shaven and their hair was worn loose down their backs. They wore golden collars, armlets, and bracelets, and some wore golden bands covering most of their calves.

Minoan women's dress was far more elaborate. They wore brightly colored dresses, with full, flounced skirts, falling in many layers to the ground. The short-sleeved tunic that covered the top of the body had a tight-fitting bodice, cut very low to leave the breasts bare. Minoan women wore golden necklaces and bracelets and left their hair long and loose. They wore tall, conical hats, or more often just a simple headband.

Myceneans

Around 1650 BCE the Greek kingdom of Mycenae, in the northeastern Peloponnese, grew very powerful. Mycenae was ruled by several kings, each of whom had his own palace. Inside the palaces were workshops for potters, weavers, and metalworkers, as well as splendid rooms for the royal family. The Myceneans were a warlike people, but they were also great sailors and traders, who imported tin to make bronze for weapons, and gold and amber to make jewelry.

Palace Dress

In the great halls of their brightly painted palaces, the Mycenean kings and queens held lavish feasts. Kings and nobles wore simple kilts with patterned borders, and usually left their chests bare. Men wore their hair loose, hanging around their shoulders, and held in place by a simple headband.

Mycenean women wore multicolored dresses, with flared, tiered skirts, and close-fitting, low-cut bodices. Their hair was loosely bound with colorful ribbons, while some locks hung down around their faces. Women wore gold and amber necklaces and bracelets, while men had golden armlets.

Beauty Routine

The famous beauty Helen of Troy was a Mycenean queen, and surviving murals show that the women of Mycenae were graceful and stylish, with artfully arranged hair. There is evidence that both women and men spent time and care on their appearance. The Myceneans produced perfumed oils, which they stored in elegant jars. Some oil was traded by merchants, but a certain quantity was kept for use at home. Inside the palaces were small stone tubs, and part of a lady's beauty routine would probably have involved soaking in a tub and then rubbing scented oil into her skin.

Both men and women in the Mycenean cities cared a great deal for their appearance, and the women were famous for their beauty.

Mycenean Warriors

War was a central part of Mycenean life. Kings and nobles trained for battle, and musicians sang songs about great victories. When a Mycenean city went to war, the king and his nobles rode in battle chariots, while the ordinary soldiers marched on foot.

Most of the army wore simple kilts and relied for their protection on helmets and shields. Helmets were usually fairly plain—a pointed bronze cap with flaps for the ears, topped by a flowing horsehair plume. The king, however, wore a helmet with a curved horn at the front. One remarkable helmet has been found that was originally constructed from dozens of boars' tusks laid side by side.

Shields were made from ox hide stretched over a wooden frame. Some shields were shaped like a solid figure eight, while others, known as "tower shields," were tall and rectangular and bowed in at the sides. Occasionally, a warrior wore a complete suit of armor made from bronze, but these were very heavy and rigid, and probably uncomfortable to wear.

Warriors fought with shields, swords, and daggers, and some of these weapons were beautifully decorated. One dagger found in a king's grave has a solid gold hilt and a blade inlaid with a scene in gold, silver, and copper, showing leopards hunting in the forest.

The golden death mask of an early Mycenean king, found by the archeologist Heinrich Schliemann.

Death Mask

The Myceneans created gleaming golden death masks for their kings. The masks were made by beating a sheet of gold over a carved wooden mold, and the sheet was then laid over the face of the dead ruler in his tomb. The most famous of these masks was discovered by the archaeologist Heinrich Schliemann in the 1870s. At first Schliemann believed that he had found the body of King Agamemnon of Troy, one of the major figures in Homer's *Iliad*, but it was later proved that the mask belonged to one of the earliest Mycenean kings.

Most Mycenean warriors did not wear body armor, but relied on their large shields for protection.

Classical Greece

By around 800 BCE the ancient Greeks were living in city-states. There were around three hundred city-states in total, but the two most powerful ones were Athens, in eastern-central Greece, and Sparta, in the south. Gradually, Athens gained in wealth and power, and by the fifth century BCE it had become the center of a thriving Greek civilization.

Ancient Greek society had an elite of wealthy, well-educated people. They created fine art and great buildings, studied mathematics and medicine, and discussed political ideas. There were also priests, soldiers, farmers, traders, and merchants. The lowest class, comprising about a quarter of the population, were slaves.

Making Clothes

Most women in ancient Greece knew how to spin wool and weave it into cloth, and a Greek wife was expected to provide all the cloth for her family. Some women did all of their household spinning and weaving themselves, but rich women often had slaves to do the work instead. One famous example of a virtuous Greek woman is Penelope, the wife of the hero Odysseus, who kept busy with her weaving for twenty years, while Odysseus was away on his adventures!

Once the wool was spun, it could be colored using natural dyes made from plants, insects, and shellfish. Women wove their thread on a tall, upright loom and sometimes included

Arachne the Weaver

Spinning and weaving were so important in ancient Greece that many myths and stories grew up about them. One story told the legend of Arachne, a very skilled weaver, who was turned into a spider by the goddess Athena because she dared to challenge Athena to a weaving contest.

patterned borders in their cloth. Geometric shapes were very popular, and mythological creatures also featured in borders. Greek clothes were usually made from wool, although some women wove thread from flax to make linen cloth. From the fifth century BCE onward, a few very rich people wore garments made from imported silk or cotton.

A woman weaving woolen cloth on a vertical loom. Most women in ancient Greece wove the cloth for their household.

Fashion in Ancient Greece

In the warm, dry climate of Greece, people did not need many clothes. Both men and women wore a simple tunic, and added a cloak for cooler weather. Tunics and cloaks were held in place by pins or brooches, which could be plain or very elaborate. Usually people went barefoot, but sometimes they wore simple leather sandals.

The basic dress for women was the chiton. It was made from a single piece of rectangular cloth, fastened at the shoulders and left open at one side. A girdle was also tied at the waist to hold the chiton in place. There were two main styles of chiton. The Doric chiton was a sleeveless tunic, while the Ionic chiton had elbow-length sleeves, which were fastened at intervals across the shoulders. Over the chiton, women wore a himation. This was a rectangular wrap, which could vary in size and weight, from a light scarf to a warm traveling cloak.

Most Greek men wore a simple tunic sewn up at the side and fastened with a pin or brooch on one or both shoulders. Young men wore their tunics short, while older men and nobles had ankle-length robes.

Craftsmen, farmers, and slaves often wore a loincloth. Sometimes men wore a himation, which they wrapped around the body with one end thrown over one shoulder. This could be worn on its own or as a second garment over a tunic.

Jewelry

The Greeks liked to wear delicate earrings, bracelets, and necklaces. Wealthy Greeks wore jewelry made from gold, silver, and ivory, while the poorer people's jewelry was made from bronze, lead, and bone. Jewelers sometimes added enamel for color, but precious stones were only used at the end of the Greek period.

This impressive necklace would have been worn by a wealthy woman. It is made from solid gold.

A couple exchanging gifts, painted on a Greek vase. The wife wears a chiton while her husband wears a flowing robe with the end draped over his shoulder.

Hairstyles

In the early Greek period, both men and women wore their hair long and loose, held in place by a simple headband. However, from around 500 BCE onward, men's hair became much shorter, and their beards were neatly trimmed, while women usually wore their hair up, bound by several ribbons and scarves. From around 300 BCE men shaved off their beards and wore their hair cropped close to their heads. Meanwhile, female hairstyles became extremely elaborate, and women often waved or curled their hair.

Beauty Care

Women in ancient Greece spent a lot of time and effort making themselves look beautiful. They would bathe frequently and rub perfumed oils into their skin to prevent it from drying out. Women also used oil on their hair to make it shine. Some women dyed their hair and wore wigs or false hairpieces, while others used padding to improve their figure, or wore thick-soled sandals to make themselves look taller. Many Greek women wore makeup. They whitened their skin with special creams, darkened their eyebrows, and used rouge on their cheeks.

Looking and smelling good was very important to the Greeks. Here, a wealthy woman massages oil into her hair, while her servant holds the oil jar.

Spartan women

In the warlike city-state of Sparta, women looked and behaved very differently from their counterparts in the rest of Greece. Spartan women were encouraged to spend most of their time outside, exercising and playing sports to make sure that they had robust, healthy babies. Statues of Spartan women and girls show that they were very strong and muscular. Usually they wore a knee-length dress, with a loose skirt to allow plenty of movement. One statue even shows a Spartan girl wearing a thigh-length tunic with a high slit in one side.

Greeks at War

This detail from a Roman mosaic shows Alexander the Great dressed in the armor of a Macedonian general. Alexander wears a metal breastplate with wide shoulder straps, and a lightweight cloak fastened at the neck. His breastplate has a decoration in the form of a head—possibly the god of war.

The ancient Greeks were often at war. For eleven years they fought against the Persians, and there was also a long war between the rival city-states of Athens and Sparta. In 338 BCE the Greeks were conquered by their northern neighbor, the kingdom of Macedonia, led by King Philip II. When Philip died in 336, his son, Alexander the Great, became the leader of the Greek army and led a force of Macedonians and Greeks on a campaign to win a vast empire in Asia and the Middle East.

Each of the main fighting groups— the Greeks (led by the city of Athens), the Spartans, and the Macedonians—had their own distinctive battle dress.

Greek Hoplites

The backbone of the Greek army was its company of heavily armed footsoldiers, known as hoplites. Hoplites fought with a long spear and a sword and carried a large circular shield made from bronze, wood, and leather, with a bold design painted on it. They wore a short tunic and their upper body was protected by a bronze and leather

A Question of Dress

After Alexander the Great had defeated the king of Persia in 331 BCE, he took control of the great Persian Empire. During this period the chroniclers relate that Alexander abandoned his traditional Macedonian dress and adopted instead the dress of the Persians, wearing a loose tunic and pants (see page 25). This infuriated Alexander's Macedonian generals, who were intensely proud of their kingdom's military history, which they saw as represented by their dress.

breastplate. Bronze leg guards, known as greaves, covered the soldiers' calves, and they wore sturdy leather sandals on their feet. The hoplites had magnificent bronze helmets with a horsehair crest and flaps to protect the sides of the face.

Running in Armor

The ancient Greeks loved to hold athletic competitions, in which men competed against each other in sports such as jumping, boxing, and wrestling. The most famous competition of all was the Olympic Games. Most Olympic sports were performed by naked athletes, but in one running race the competitors had to wear heavy armor. Each of the runners wore a bronze helmet and greaves and carried a heavy shield. The origins of this race probably lay in the strict training of the Greek hoplites.

Spartan Warriors

All the men of Sparta were full-time soldiers. At the age of seven, boys were taken from their mothers to begin their military training. Spartan warriors dressed in a distinctive way, with long, scarlet cloaks and helmets which covered almost all of the face. The Spartan soldiers also let their hair grow long, so that it streamed out from under their helmets. The overall effect could be very fearsome when they advanced *en masse* in battle.

Alexander's Armor

Alexander the Great was one of the finest generals the world has ever known. When he led the Greeks into battle, he wore the traditional armor of his native kingdom of Macedonia: a short-sleeved battle tunic with a metal breastplate and a skirt and sleeves made from metal strips. Alexander rode an enormous charger and fought with a long sword. On his feet he had calf-length boots and he wore a purple cloak to show his royal status. In most of the surviving statues and mosaics, Alexander is bareheaded, but one statue shows him as a fierce conqueror, wearing a lion's head with its paws tied under his chin.

Greek hoplites depicted on a vase from the sixth century BCE. The Hoplites all wear splendid, crested headdresses and carry circular shields—each with its own distinctive design.

Chapter 5: The Roman Empire

Ancient Romans

In this mosaic from the fourth century BCE the Roman poet Virgil is flanked by two muses (goddesses of inspiration). Virgil wears a toga looped over one shoulder.

The Roman Empire began as a small community of farmers living on the banks of the Tiber River in Italy. Gradually, the farming villages grew into a town and then into a city.

A Roman woman dressed in stola (dress) and palla (shawl). The Romans used hand-mirrors made from highly-polished metal.

palla —

stola —

At first the city of Rome was ruled by kings, but in 509 BCE the last king was driven out and Rome became a republic ruled by two elected consuls, who were advised by a senate. In 45 BCE a general named Julius Caesar seized power, but he was soon assassinated, and a period of conflict followed until Augustus took control in 27 BCE. Augustus was the first Roman emperor, and the empire lasted for the next four hundred years.

Augustus and his successors conquered vast areas of land, creating an empire that stretched from Britain in the north to North Africa in the south. Wherever the Romans conquered, they established the Roman way of life, building fine cities with temples, baths, and theaters. Governors were sent from Rome to rule over the provinces, and many of the conquered peoples adopted Roman ways, even dressing like the Romans.

Making Clothes

Most Roman clothes were made from wool, which was spun and woven by hand at home or in a workshop. In towns and cities, Romans took their woolen cloth to the fuller's workshop to be cleaned and treated before it was made into clothes. First, the cloth was stiffened by soaking it in urine, and then it was cleaned by rubbing it with a kind of clay. After this, the cloth was beaten, stretched, and bleached. Fullers also cleaned and mended clothes for the richer people.

Sometimes the Romans had clothes made from linen, which came from Egypt. The wealthiest wore clothes made of cotton from India and silk from China.

Togas and Tunics

The basic garment for men was a simple, belted tunic made from two rectangles of wool stitched together. Tunics were usually made of unbleached wool and reached to the knees. Under their tunics men wore a loincloth made from a strip of wool or linen. They also had a simple cloak, which could be wrapped around them or fastened with a brooch at the neck.

Important men wore a toga over their tunic. This was a very long strip of woolen cloth, wrapped around the body and draped over one shoulder. However, the toga was very heavy and awkward to wear, so it was only worn for special occasions. Togas were usually plain white, but those worn by senators had a broad purple border. Until they were sixteen, boys from wealthy families wore a white toga with a narrow purple border.

Roman Rings

Roman men and women wore a lot of rings. Rich people had rings made from gold and silver and set with precious stones such as emeralds, pearls, or amber. Less wealthy people wore rings made from bronze. Often a ring held a gemstone engraved with a pattern that could be used as a seal.

Women's Clothing

Roman women wore a long, belted, sleeveless dress called a stola. Over this was a large, rectangular shawl, known as a palla, which could be worn draped around the shoulders or looped over the head like a hood. Under the stola women wore a loincloth and sometimes a simple leather bra. Girls wore white until they were married, but after this they often wore brightly colored dresses.

This young woman wears simple gold earrings in her ears, while her carefully curled hair is held in place by a delicate lattice-work cap.

Hair Care

Most Roman men kept their hair short, either combed forward or curled. They were usually clean-shaven, although the emperor Hadrian (reigned 117–138 CE) started a fashion for beards. Most men began the day by visiting the barber's shop for a shave, and some had the hair removed from their arms and legs as well. This could be a painful experience because barbers did not use soap or oil.

During the period of the republic, most women wore their hair tied in simple buns at the back of their heads, but by the time of the empire some very elaborate styles had developed. Wealthy women's hair was curled and braided and piled into elaborate styles, held in place with dozens of pins.

For special celebrations, wealthy women wore wigs, and brides wore several hairpieces for their weddings. Some women cut off their slaves' hair and had it made into wigs or hairpieces. Others bought wigs made from imported hair. Black hair came from Asia, while blond and red hair was imported from northern Europe. Some Romans used a brown hair dye made from walnut shells and wild onions. Others tried to prevent their hair from going gray by applying a paste of earthworms and herbs!

Makeup

Most wealthy Roman women relied on cosmetics to make themselves look beautiful, and slaves devoted hours each morning to making up their mistresses. It was very fashionable in Roman times for women to look pale, so women whitened their faces and arms with powdered chalk or a poisonous mixture made from lead. They darkened their eyebrows and eyelashes with soot and wore eye shadow made from ash or saffron. Color was added to lips and cheeks using red ocher, plant dye, or even the sediment of red wine.

False Teeth

Many Romans suffered from tooth decay, and sometimes dentists took drastic action. They extracted rotten teeth and supplied false ones to fill the gaps. False teeth were made from ivory or bone and were attached to a gold band that would not rust.

As well as applying makeup, Roman women liked to treat their skin with a variety of creams. They applied facials of bread soaked in milk and even used a cream made from crushed snails. Perfumes were very popular, and women kept their cosmetics and scent in delicate glass pots and bottles.

Roman Baths

Very few Roman houses had bathrooms, so most people visited the public baths. However, a visit to the baths was much more than a chance to get clean. Like modern health clubs, Roman baths offered the chance for a total exercise and beauty routine. Many Romans began their visit to the baths with a session in the exercise yards, where they could practice weightlifting, wrestling, or ball games. This could be followed by a period in the sudatorium—a hot, steamy room, like a modern-day sauna.

In the *caldarium*, or hot bath, the Romans smeared their bodies with perfumed oil and then scraped off the dirt with a curved stick called a strigil. After this they visited the *tepidarium*, a lukewarm pool where they could cool down, and then perhaps enjoy a massage. The whole experience ended with a refreshing dip in the *frigidarium*—the unheated, outdoor swimming pool.

A surviving Roman bath from the city of Bath, in southern England. (Only the lower section dates from Roman times.)

Roman Actors

Throughout the Roman Empire, companies of actors performed plays to entertain the people. These plays were usually solemn tragedies about heroes and gods, or knockabout comedies about ordinary people. All the parts were taken by men, and the actors wore distinctive costumes and masks to help the audience understand their roles in the play. Roman drama had its origins in the plays of the ancient Greeks, and Greek and Roman actors wore very similar costumes and masks.

Costumes

Roman plays were usually performed in huge, outdoor theaters, with rows of seats built in a high circle around a central stage. Because of the vast size of these theaters, the actors had to be easily visible. They wore exaggerated masks and large wigs, and many actors added extra padding under their costumes to give themselves more bulk. The actors playing women used special padding to give them a more female shape.

Costumes were fairly simple and usually consisted of a tunic and cloak, which were short for men and long for those playing women. The colors of an actor's clothes helped to identify his role in the drama, so tragic characters wore dark robes, while happy characters had brightly colored costumes. As well as the individual actors, most plays featured a chorus—a group of actors who all spoke at once. Members of the chorus also wore costumes and sometimes even dressed as animals or birds.

Two Roman actors' masks from a mosaic. The mask on the left would be worn by a comic character, while the one on the right represents a pale-skinned maiden.

Masks

In addition to their costumes, the actors wore masks to help the audience recognize what kind of character they were playing. The masks had exaggerated features which showed the character's sex and age, and whether they were humans or gods. Female masks were much paler than male ones and had bigger eyes. There were special masks for recognizable character types such as the "wise old man," the "fool," the "innocent maiden," and "the scheming slave." During the course of a performance, an actor might wear several masks, swapping perhaps from a smiling to an angry mask to indicate that his character's mood had changed.

Actors' masks were usually made from stiffened, painted linen, and they were lightweight, but very hot. They had holes for the eyes and a very large hole for the mouth, which helped to amplify the actor's voice so that he could be heard by everyone in the theater.

Actors' Shoes

Ancient Greek and Roman actors sometimes wore special shoes to make them seem taller. These shoes were made from wood and had thick soles and a high heel. The shoes had no left or right and looked the same from both sides.

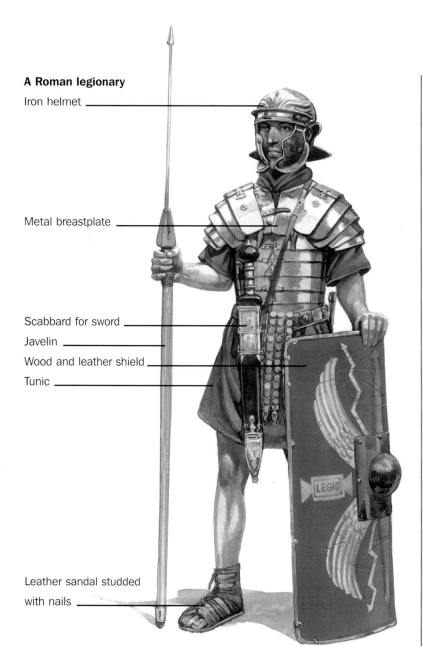

A Roman legionary

Iron helmet

Metal breastplate

Scabbard for sword

Javelin

Wood and leather shield

Tunic

Leather sandal studded
with nails

The Roman Army

In the early republic, Rome did not have a professional army, because in times of war, all male citizens were expected to fight. The men had to provide their own weapons and equipment and then return home when the fighting was over. By the time of the empire, however, the Roman army had become an extremely efficient fighting force. Soldiers were well-paid professionals who wore regulation armor and weapons.

The Roman army was divided into legions—groups of around six thousand men. Within the legions, most men fought as legionaries, or foot soldiers, while a smaller group of mounted soldiers formed the cavalry. Marching at the head of the legion was the *aquilifer* or standard-bearer. Roman legionaries wore short tunics and leather sandals studded with nails. They fought with daggers, swords, and javelins and carried a large wood and leather shield. An iron helmet protected their head and

Useful Shields

While the shields of the Roman cavalry were flat and oval, the legionaries' shields were rectangular in shape and bowed outward. The shields were made in this distinctive shape so that the legionaries could form a cunning formation. Groups of soldiers advancing toward the enemy locked their shields together to form a solid barrier that covered the soldiers' heads and also protected the front and sides of the group. This well-protected shape was known as the testudo, or tortoise, and it allowed the legionaries to approach very close to the enemy before launching their attack.

they also wore a breastplate made from metal strips.

Standard-bearers led their legion into battle, so they had to be easy to spot. As well as their basic armor, they wore a dramatic headdress made from the head and front paws of a lion, and carried a tall staff topped by a golden emblem of an eagle.

Another dramatic figure on the battlefield was the *cornicene*, or horn player. He blew battle signals, using a large, circular trumpet, and wore a striking costume made from a bear's head and skin.

Each Roman legion was divided into many smaller groups, and each group had its own commander. The most important commander was the legate, who was in charge of the whole legion and wore a golden helmet topped with eagle's wings. The least important was the centurion, who commanded a group of around eighty men. The centurion wore similar armor to the legionary, but his shins were protected by metal plates called greaves, and he wore a plumed helmet on his head.

Gladiators

The Roman emperors paid for dramatic and bloodthirsty shows to entertain the people of the city. Known as "the games," these shows were held in massive stone stadiums, such as the Colosseum in Rome. One of the most popular games was the gladiator fight. Gladiators were slaves, criminals, or prisoners of war, who were forced to fight each other to the death.

Most gladiators fought with very short swords. They wore simple loincloths and went bare-chested, although they did wear a helmet and carry a shield. One type of gladiator, called a *retiarius*, fought with a net and wore no armor at all.

This mosaic shows two scenes of gladiators fighting. The figure on the left in both scenes is a retiarius, who fights with a net.

Barbarians and Celts

Although the Romans were very successful at conquering the peoples of Europe, there were some tribes who resisted them. The Roman army fought constant battles with the Celtic people, while tribes of Germanic people from northeastern Europe launched frequent attacks on the empire's borders.

Barbarian Warriors

By the third century CE attacks on the Roman Empire by Germanic tribes were growing more serious.

A Frankish warrior, armed with his throwing axe, known as a *francisca*.

The Romans called these tribes "barbarians" and fought fiercely to keep them out of their lands. Eventually, however, Rome was invaded by barbarians, and in 476 the Roman Empire collapsed in western Europe.

Rome was threatened by many warlike tribes, but one of the most terrifying were the Franks, who originally came from Germany. Frankish warriors carried circular wooden shields and fought with spears and lethal throwing axes called *franciscas*. They wore rough coats made from furs, short tunics and leggings, and boots cross-laced around their calves. However, the most striking aspect of the warriors' appearance was their hair. This was worn in a pigtail at the front, and shaved at the back with an extra topknot of hair sprouting from the top of the head.

Celtic People

The people known as the Celts were made up of many different tribes, but they all shared the same language and way of life. The Celtic culture began in Austria around 800 BCE, and the Celts gradually spread across most of Europe, settling as far north as Scotland and as far south as Turkey. As the Roman Empire grew, the Celts fought hard to defend their lands, but in the end most of them were conquered. However, Celtic culture survived in Ireland and remote parts of Scotland and Wales, while in Cornwall and Brittany some Celtic traditions remained.

Celtic Dress

Celtic men wore short, belted tunics and baggy pants tied at the ankle with strips of leather, while women wore long dresses with belts. Both men and women often wore chunky neckbands, known as torcs, made from twisted bands of gold.

In battle, Celtic warriors wore bronze helmets, which were sometimes crowned with horns or animal ornaments. They carried bronze shields, fought with spears, and blew on tall war trumpets decorated with animal heads. To make themselves appear more intimidating to their enemies, some Celtic warriors stripped to the waist and painted their bodies with swirling patterns, using a blue dye called woad. They also combed lime through their hair to make it stand up in spikes.

Celtic warriors usually wore thick woolen clothes with bold patterns of checks and plaids.

Celtic Metalwork

The Celts were skilled metalworkers who made strong weapons and tools. They also created beautiful cups, shields, and items of jewelry from bronze, silver, and gold. Some of these objects, dating from around two thousand years ago, are decorated with intricate swirling patterns, and the same sort of patterns appeared much later in Celtic medieval art.

A Celtic bronze shield dating from around 350 BCE.

Checks and Plaids

Celtic clothes were woven from wool and dyed bright colors, and often featured patterns of stripes, checks, and very simple plaids. These simple designs were probably the origin of the traditional plaid patterns later used in Scottish kilts.

Chapter 6: Peoples of the South and East

Ancient India

India has a rich early history. The Indus valley civilization, which flourished between 2600 and 2000 BCE, was larger than any other empire of the time. The Aryan people, who arrived in India around 1500 BCE, introduced the religion of Hinduism, while Buddhism also began in India around 500 BCE. The Gupta Empire of the fourth to the sixth centuries CE is famous for its painting, music, and dance.

People of the Indus Valley

The first civilization in India grew up around the valley of the Indus River around 3500 BCE. Within a thousand years there were over a hundred towns and cities in the Indus valley. The farmers there were the first people to grow cotton and weave it into cloth for clothes. Meanwhile, in the towns and cities, metalworkers and bead makers made headbands, armlets, and necklaces. Beads for necklaces were made from gold, clay, and semiprecious stones. Some pottery beads were modeled in the form of tiny animals.

Clothes for Castes

The Aryan people, who arrived in India around 1500 BCE, introduced a caste system in which people were divided into different classes according to the jobs they did. Children always belonged to the same caste as their parents, and each caste wore different kinds of clothes. The main castes were: the workers, who wore a simple tunic and turban; the merchants, who dressed in more colorful robes and wore golden jewelry; the warriors and kings, who wore magnificently patterned robes and turbans and masses of jewelry; and the priests and scholars, who usually dressed very simply in a loincloth, with their hair knotted behind their head.

Buddhist Monks

Around 528 BCE Prince Siddhartha Gautama gave up his worldly riches and became the Buddha, a wandering holy man who dressed very simply and had almost no possessions. The Buddha attracted many followers who wished to live like him, and he gave precise instructions about their robes. These robes have been worn by Buddhist monks from the sixth century BCE right up to the present day.

Buddhist monks have a "triple robe," which consists of: a waistcloth, wrapped around the body like a

Buddhist monks today still wear the same traditional saffron robes that they wore in the sixth century BCE.

sarong; a robe; and an outer robe, which is only worn in cold weather. Monks' robes can be dyed from roots and tubers, plants, bark, leaves, flowers, and fruits, and these natural substances produce a range of colors from deep red to yellow. The most common color for Buddhist robes is a yellowish-orange, or saffron.

The Gupta Empire

The Gupta emperors ruled from 320 to 550 CE, and encouraged art, science, and trade. Textiles were a major source of wealth for the empire, and large quantities of silk, cotton, linen, and muslin (a very fine cotton) were produced to be traded abroad.

While the ordinary people in the Gupta Empire wore simple clothes made from cotton, kings, princes, and princesses had splendid clothes and jewelry. A set of famous Buddhist murals painted at Ajanta during the Guptas' rule portray a group of exquisite dancing maidens, laden with jewels. The dancers wear flowing robes of the finest muslin. Around their necks, waists, arms, and legs are strings of pearls, beads, and jewels. Some have golden, jeweled headdresses rising in points, while others are bareheaded with jewels and flowers woven into their hair.

The *Tilaka*

Ever since the Aryan period, Hindu women have worn a mark called the tilaka on their foreheads. It is usually made from a mixture of red ocher powder and sandalwood paste and is a visible sign that a person belongs to the Hindu religion. According to ancient Hindu tradition, the tilaka began in Aryan times when the bridegroom used his thumb to apply his blood to his bride's forehead as a recognition of their marriage.

Ancient China

Around 5000 BCE people began farming along the banks of the Yellow River. After a thousand years, farmers began to grow rice, and around 2700 BCE they discovered how to make silk. From that time on, wealthy people in China wore exquisite robes woven from this material.

Chinese nobles wore colorful silk robes covered with embroidery.

Making Silk

Silk thread is produced by silkworms that spin their thread into tightly bound cocoons. The ancient Chinese discovered that if they soaked these cocoons in hot water, the threads would loosen, making it possible to unwind the silk thread onto a stick. Once the thread was collected, several strands were twisted together to make threads thick enough for weaving. By creating threads of different thicknesses, the Chinese could weave a range of different silk cloths, from light gauzes to heavy brocades.

Fancy Fingernails

Around 3000 BCE wealthy people in China began to paint their fingernails. The colors used depended on rank. China's early rulers wore gold and silver nail polish, but by the time of the emperors the royal colors were red and black. Well-manicured nails were a symbol of a high social position. They emphasized the difference between the nobility and the workers, who had to labor with their hands.

These nail protectors were worn by a Chinese empress over her six-inch-long fingernails.

Silk was woven on looms to make fine cloth, but was also used for embroidery thread. The Chinese soon learned to embroider exquisite patterns onto silk cloth, often using a contrasting color. Some silk was made into beautiful clothes, and some was taken by merchants who traveled to the West, where silk sold for enormous prices. Soon, Chinese silk was so famous that the trading route that ran across Asia to Europe became known as the Silk Road.

Emperors and Nobles

In 221 BCE Qin Shi Huangdi established China's first empire. He established a pattern of living very grandly, and the emperors that followed him built magnificent palaces where they lived with their courtiers. Emperors and nobles wore wide-sleeved, flowing silk robes, which crossed over at the front and were fastened by a high belt. The robes included long, trailing sashes and were covered with embroidered designs. Emperors and nobles often wore their beards and moustaches long. Emperors had elaborate caps decorated with tassels, while nobles usually wore their hair tied in a topknot and covered with a small, silken cap.

Working Dress

The Chinese had strict rules about dress. No merchants were allowed to wear silk, and farmers and craftworkers dressed very simply. Some wore cotton loincloths, while others had loose tunics and pants. On their feet they wore sandals made from rushes or straw. In the warm, wet south, peasants working in the fields wore wide-brimmed, cone-shaped hats to protect them from the sun and rain.

Chinese Warriors

The enormous tomb of the first emperor of China contains more than seven thousand life-sized model warriors, placed there to guard his body. Made from terracotta and originally brightly painted, the warriors wear knee-length tunics. Some warriors have their hair tied in a topknot and wear a simple headband, but the officers sport elaborate bonnets with two wings at the top that tie under the chin. Some of the warriors carried real crossbows, which were set to fire if anyone dared to enter the tomb.

One of the thousands of terracotta warriors guarding the first emperor's tomb. This figure originally held a real weapon.

Ancient Japan

The earliest people in Japan lived as hunter-gatherers, hunting, fishing, and collecting nuts and berries. Then, around 500 BCE, settlers arrived from China and Korea. They brought new skills, such as metalworking and farming, and people began to live in tribes, ruled by chieftains. One tribe, called the Yamato, became more powerful than all the others, and around 500 CE they took control, becoming the first emperors of a united Japan.

Yamato Emperors and Warriors

The Yamato emperors ruled until around 700 CE. During their rule, many new ideas, such as writing and silk-making were brought over from China. People in ancient Japan probably dressed in the same way as the ancient Chinese, with farmers wearing simple tunics and pants, while richer people wore fine robes made from silk.

The best evidence for ancient Japanese costumes comes from the burial mounds of the Yamato emperors. Here, archaeologists have found bronze mirrors, bells, swords, and spears. They have also discovered clay models of warriors, placed around the burial mound to protect the emperor's body. These miniature figures are dressed completely in armor that seems to be made from metal strips. The armor consists of: a helmet with long side flaps meeting under the chin; a long, waisted jacket tied at the front with laces; and wide pants. The warriors wear gauntlets and have swords in scabbards on their belts.

A miniature terracotta soldier from a Yamato emperor's tomb.

Swords, Jewels, and Mirrors

An ancient Japanese creation myth provides some insight into the things that were considered important in early Japanese society. According to this myth, the sun goddess Amaterasu sent her grandson Ninigi to rule over Japan, giving him a sword, a jewel, and a mirror. These three gifts became symbols of the emperor's authority. They are said to be still owned by Japan's ruling family.

Australia and the Pacific

During the last Ice Age, adventurous groups of people from Southeast Asia began to journey in boats. They rowed south across the Pacific Ocean, which was much smaller than it is today because large amounts of land were covered in ice. Some people settled on islands in the South Pacific, and some reached as far as Australia. Very much later, around 750 BCE, a group called the Maoris arrived in New Zealand.

Pacific Islanders

The people who settled on the Pacific islands wore skirts made from dried grasses and necklaces made from shells, feathers, and teeth. They may have decorated their faces and bodies with body paint or tattoos, like the Maoris. They may also have worn small carvings as good-luck charms.

Australian Aboriginals

The aboriginal people of Australia first arrived on the continent around 40,000 years ago, and gradually spread out all over Australia. In the cooler regions, the aboriginals wore animal skins to keep warm, but in many parts of Australia there was no need for clothes.

The early aboriginals painted their bodies with patterns using pigments made from ochers, white clay, and charcoal. Both men and women wore a range of ornaments made from natural materials such as bark, teeth, and feathers, or carved from wood. Aboriginal hunters used boomerangs, clubs, and spears, and defended themselves with wooden shields, which were decorated with carvings or paintings.

Dreamtime Patterns

All the patterns used in aboriginal body painting have traditional meanings. They show figures and events from the Dreamtime, a period when their world was created by the Spirit Ancestors, according to aboriginal belief.

Today, some Australian aboriginals still paint their bodies with the same designs that their ancestors used thousands of years ago.

Chapter 7: People of the Americas

North America

During the last Ice Age, Asia and America were linked by a bridge of land and ice. Hunters from northern Asia followed herds of buffalo until they arrived in the northwestern tip of America. Then, very gradually, over thousands of years, people spread out all over the continent. In each area where they settled, the Native Americans established a different way of life.

Traditional Inuit dress is made entirely from animal skins and fur. It must have stayed unchanged for thousands of years.

Arctic People

By around 12,000 BCE people had settled in the frozen Arctic regions. These early ancestors of the Inuit people lived by hunting seals and walruses, fish, and birds. Like their Inuit descendants, the people of the Arctic must have used animal skins to make hooded coats, pants, mittens, and boots. They also carved ornaments from walrus tusks. A miniature ivory mask survives from around 500 BCE, which may have belonged to a chief or a priest.

Hunters of the Plains

It is thought that the first people arrived in the Great Plains area around 10,000 BCE. The people of the plains hunted buffalo for food, and hunters disguised themselves by wearing the skin of a wolf or a buffalo. Like the later people of the plains, the early buffalo hunters must have used buffalo hides to make tepees and clothes. The early plains dwellers probably also held ceremonial dances, when some of them dressed as buffalo.

Mound Builders

Around 500 BCE a people called the Adena flourished in southern Ohio. Evidence of these people, including small burial mounds, has been found in the Scioto River valley. They were succeeded around 300 BCE by the

Early Basketmakers

In the hot, sandy deserts of the southwest, people learned to weave baskets from plant fibers. From the first century CE these desert people, usually known as the Early Basketmakers, used their weaving skills to build conical homes in the sand, and also made baskets to be carried on their backs. Some baskets were lined with gum from plants so they could hold water.

These Native American buffalo hunters, painted in the nineteenth century, wear clothes made from leather and feathers. Their ancient ancestors probably dressed in a similar way, though they may not have ridden horses.

Hopewell, another great mound-building civilization, who flourished until the sixth century CE. Over time, the Hopewell people built larger burial mounds, until they had become substantial, circular burial chambers. Inside these chambers, archaeologists have found copper bracelets, necklaces made from shells and alligator teeth, wooden masks, and carved wooden pipes.

The Hopewell people were great traders who exchanged goods with tribes as far away as the Rocky Mountains and the Gulf of Mexico, and brought back copper, silver, mica, and quartz. Hopewell craftworkers made copper sheets into designs such as flying birds. They also cut out shapes, such as hands and claws, from

mica sheets. No one knows the function of these small, flat ornaments, but they may have been worn as pendants, or sewn onto clothes.

The Adena and Hopewell people probably lived in a similar way to the later tribes of the northeastern woodlands. These people were hunters and gatherers who wore loincloths, cloaks, and moccasins made from leather and decorated with dried seeds and feathers. They painted patterns on their skin and wore feathered headdresses on their heads. In their ceremonies they smoked tobacco from a carved pipe which was passed between them, and they also held dances in which some tribe members wore carved wooden masks.

The Hopewell people made fine jewelry using a wide range of natural materials. This necklace was made from pearl beads gathered from freshwater shellfish, while the pendants and earrings were fashioned from beaten copper.

South America

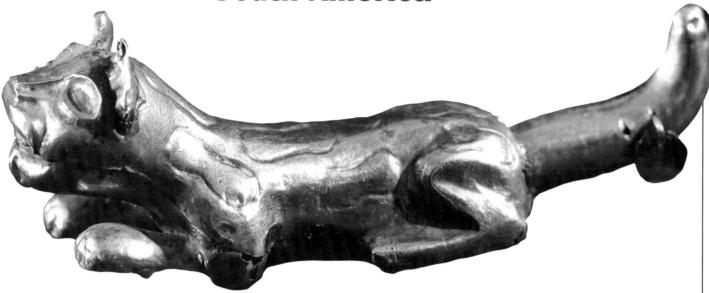

A Chavin figurine of a wild cat. This solid gold ornament may have been worn by a ruler or a priest.

The Paracas people mummified their rulers and buried them in fine woolen garments. This Paracas burial cloak and headdress were made from dyed and embroidered wool.

People of Peru

People began to settle on the rocky coast of Peru around 12,000 BCE. At first, they survived by catching shellfish and crabs and gathering nuts and berries, but by about 2000 BCE they had learned to grow crops. The Peruvian farmers grew maize, squash, beans, and potatoes, and also cotton for spinning and weaving. They kept llamas, alpacas, and guinea pigs for their meat and wool, which was used to weave blankets and cloaks.

Between 1800 and 900 BCE the Chavin people created the first civilization in South America. They were skilled stoneworkers who built huge temples filled with carvings of their fierce animal gods. The Chavin people settled in the long coastal strip which is present-day Peru and influenced the culture of the whole area. Chavin culture disappeared around 200 BCE, but other groups grew up, including the Paracas cultures in the south, and the Moche in the north.

Chavin Gold

Little evidence remains of Chavin clothing, but they were the first people in the Americas to work gold. Chavin goldsmiths made intricate figurines and pendants covered with expressive carving. These ornaments show a range of animal spirits, including jaguars, eagles, alligators, crabs, and shellfish. In addition to the figurines, wide gold collars and pectorals have also been found in Chavin temples. All of these splendid ornaments were probably worn by Chavin rulers and priests.

Paracas Cloth

The Paracas people, who flourished in the southern Andes from around 600 BCE to 400 CE, are famous for their weaving and embroidery. Weavers used fine alpaca wool to make spectacular cloaks and burial cloths in a range of vivid colors. Some surviving Paracas cloth has geometric figures and motifs woven into it, while some is decorated with embroidered designs. The cloth is brightly colored with dyes, including turquoise, scarlet, and jade green. Designs include a range of animal motifs, such as alpacas, birds of prey, jaguars, and snakes. Sometimes weavers combined the forms of several creatures into a complex intertwined design. Semi-human deities are also shown, displaying a mixture of human and animal features.

One surviving Paracas textile has a recurrent design of flying figures, apparently wearing ceremonial dress.

The figures wear short, decorated kilts with elaborately patterned belts. Around their ankles are feathered leg bands, and hanging around their necks are square, woven bags. Each figure carries a baton and a fan, and wears a simple headdress of two horizontal bands topped by a design of an animal's face.

A Paracas llama-wool textile used to wrap the body of a mummified ruler. The figures on this embroidery may represent warrior priests.

Sacred Gold

All the ancient people of the Andes worshiped the sun god, and gold was especially prized because it was associated with the sun god's life-giving power. For their special ceremonies, Moche lords were festooned with golden jewelry and also wore a cotton cloak covered with gilded plates. When a Moche lord appeared on the top of his pyramid, glittering in all his finery, he personified the god of the sun.

This "stirrup vase" made by the Moche people shows a laughing man wearing a simple cotton cap.

Moche Lords

Between 200 and 800 CE, the Moche lords ruled over a coastal kingdom in northern Peru. Most of the Moche people lived in small farming or fishing villages clustered around tall pyramids where the lords had their palaces. The Moche lords conducted solemn ceremonies and led their warriors into battle. They also supervised the work of skilled craftspeople who worked in clay, textiles, and metals.

Moche Jewelry

Metalworkers smelted gold, silver, and copper in small furnaces and used stone hammers to flatten the metal into thin sheets. From these they fashioned gleaming headdresses, face masks, nose rings, earrings, pectorals, and pendants. Moche jewelry was often covered with fine engravings and sometimes inlaid with turquoise, shell, and lapis lazuli.

Portraits in Clay

Moche lords commissioned skilled potters to make bowls, pots, and vases, painted with designs in red, white, and earth colors. Many of the pots feature painted figures and scenes, while some "stirrup vases" take the form of human figures. Moche pottery reveals a fantastic range of costumes: lords adorned with face paint and wearing feathered headdresses, warriors in patterned battle tunics and headdresses, and ordinary people in cotton tunics and caps. One surviving pot even shows a man washing his hair with coca leaves.

Central America

Olmecs

The first major Central American civilization emerged around 1500 BCE in the humid, swampy lands around the Gulf of Mexico. Here, the Olmec people built a series of ceremonial sites on low hills. The two major sites were San Lorenzo and La Venta. Each contained a complex of temple platforms and pyramid mounds and a court for a sacred ball game.

The Olmecs were the first of a series of peoples that flourished in Central America, and many aspects of their culture were adopted by later groups, including the Maya people (see pages 58 and 59).

Olmec Carvings

Olmec craftspeople created masks and figurines from jade, obsidian, and serpentine, which were possibly worn as pendants. These carvings featured eagles, serpents, and jaguars, and also semi-human figures with snarling jaguar faces.

Olmec sculptors also carved a set of giant stone heads, which are probably portraits of leaders. Each of them wears a distinctive helmet-like headdress with straps around the ears. Some have a decorated badge at the center of the forehead.

Sacred Ball Game

As part of their religion, the Olmecs played a sacred ball game on a stone court. Players hit a rubber ball with their arms, hands, and hips, and at the end of the game one team was put to death.

Carvings show that the Olmec ball-game players wore a protective helmet, similar to the headdress of their rulers. They also wore a large chest ornament and a high-cut loincloth with a wide, padded waistband. Later, the Maya also played a sacred ball game, and their players wore a similar costume.

A colossal stone head from San Lorenzo, Mexico. Carved heads like these were probably intended as portraits of rulers.

The Olmecs and the Maya played a sacred ball game. Players had special loincloths and helmets and wore large ornaments on their chests.

This painting shows a range of Maya costumes. The figure on the left carrying a bundle is probably an ordinary farmer. The two central figures may be courtiers, while the dark figure in the feathered headdress (top left) is a warrior.

Maya

Around 300 BCE the Maya people started building stone cities deep in the rainforests of Central America. Each Maya city was filled with temples and palaces and was ruled by a powerful king. The palaces and pyramids of the Maya cities were covered with sculptures of their gods and rulers. The Maya also produced painted pots and manuscripts, which offer a wealth of evidence about the way they looked and dressed.

Maya Beauty

The Maya people had flattened foreheads that sloped backwards, giving their faces an oval, egg-like shape. This shape was achieved by binding the skulls of babies while their bones were still soft. Maya nobles also filed their teeth into different shapes, and built up the bridge of their nose with clay to make a long ridge that extended right up to the middle of the forehead. Hair was sometimes worn over the forehead and cut in uneven, squared-off locks.

Kings and Queens

Maya kings and queens wore amazing costumes. The kings wore patterned tunics with elaborate belts and large pectorals featuring images of their gods. They also wore decorated armbands, tasseled leg bands, and pendulous earrings. On their heads they had a towering headdress that frequently featured an animal's head. The Maya queens' clothes were equally dramatic. They wore long cloaks and dresses, heavy golden neck collars, intricate earrings, and tall and elaborate crowns.

Ordinary people wore a basic, cotton loincloth, and a simple cap on their heads. They also wore chunky beads, armbands, and earrings.

Maya Warriors

In battle, Maya warriors dressed to scare their enemies. They wore huge, spiky headdresses and went into battle shouting, blowing long trumpets, and pulling frightening faces. Warriors defended themselves with shields and fought with long spears, but they aimed to take their prisoners alive, rather than kill them. The fiercest warriors of all were the jaguar knights. Their tunics, headdresses, shields, and spears were all decorated with jaguar skin, and their headdresses were shaped like a jaguar's head.

Imitating the Gods

The Maya worshiped dozens of gods and held many ceremonies to please them. As part of these ceremonies, priests and kings wore costumes and headdresses representing their gods. The most important of all the gods was the sun god, and when the Maya kings were buried, they wore a mask showing the sun god's face. These royal burial masks were usually made of jade, the Mayan's most precious material, which they associated with everlasting life.

Quetzal Feathers

Most of the ancient peoples of Central America worshiped the serpent god Quetzalcoatl. Quetzalcoatl was half snake and half Quetzal bird, and the feathers of the Quetzal bird were considered sacred. Like other Central American peoples, the Maya used the long, green tail feathers of the Quetzal bird in the headdresses of their rulers and priests.

A Maya warrior painted on a vase. This portrait shows very clearly the backward-sloping forehead which the Maya people considered very beautiful.

Timeline

c. 114,000–c. 30,000 People begin to wear clothes. Prehistoric people make simple clothes from animal skins, wear jewelry made from shells and teeth, and use body paint for ceremonies.

c. 29,000 The earliest evidence of woven cloth (probably from grasses) dates from this time.

c. 24,000 Twine nets are first woven.

c. 10,000 Jewelry is made from pottery and semiprecious stones.

c. 9000–6000 Farmers in Iraq learn to spin wool and weave it into simple tunics.

c. 8000 Linen is first woven in Europe; hemp is first used for making cloth in China.

c. 5000 Cotton is spun and woven into cloth in Central America.

c. 3500 Cotton manufacture develops in India.

c. 3100 The Egyptian civilization begins. The ancient Egyptians learn to weave linen clothes from flax. Many Egyptians wear elaborate jewelry, wigs, and makeup.

c. 3000 The ancient Sumerians learn to make necklaces, daggers, and helmets from copper, silver, and gold. Bronze is discovered, and used for making axes, spears, and strong helmets.

c. 2700 Silk-making begins in China. The ancient Chinese weave elaborate silk robes. They also export silk to Europe along the Silk Road.

c. 2600 The people of the Indus valley grow cotton and use it to make clothes.

c. 1500 The Chavin people are the first civilization in the Americas to discover gold. Chavin goldsmiths make golden ornaments and collars.

c. 1200 The Phoenicians make a purple dye which is sold around the Mediterranean. They also discover how to blow glass and make glass beads and ornaments.

c. 600 The Paracas people of the Andes create elaborate woven costumes.

c. 520 The Persians start to build their empire. Persian warriors wear pants for riding.

c. 500 The ancient Greek civilization begins to flourish. Greek soldiers wear strong protective armor.

c. 300 The Mayans start building stone cities. Maya rulers and warriors wear elaborate headdresses.

27 The Roman Empire begins. Roman styles of dress spread across the Middle East and Europe.

Glossary

alloy A mixture of two or more metals.

alpaca A goatlike animal that comes from South America. Alpacas have long, shaggy hair that is used to make fine wool.

amulet An ornament or piece of jewelry that is believed to bring its owner good luck.

appliqué A method of decorating fabric in which pieces of a different material are sewn onto the fabric.

armlet A band that is worn around the upper arm.

baton A long, thin stick sometimes carried by a warrior.

bodice The tight-fitting upper part of a woman's dress.

boomerang A curved stick that is thrown through the air and returns to its thrower if it misses its target. Boomerangs are used by aboriginal hunters in Australia.

braid A length of hair that has been divided into three strands and twisted together.

braided Divided into strands and twisted together.

brocade A rich fabric with a raised pattern woven into it. Brocades often have raised patterns made from gold or silver threads.

coca leaves Leaves from the coca plant, which grows in the Andes Mountains.

cochineal insect A Mexican insect whose crushed body produces a bright crimson dye.

enamel A shiny, glasslike substance that can be produced in a range of colors and is often used to decorate metal objects.

fez A cone-shaped hat without a brim.

flail An instrument with a handle and a free-swinging end, used for beating corn or as a whip.

flounced Gathered to create a ruffle. A flounced skirt is usually made up of several layers of gathered fabric.

fluted Decorated with regular vertical grooves or dips.

fuller Someone who makes and treats cloth.

gauntlet A heavy glove with a long cuff.

gauze A very thin woven cloth that is almost transparent.

gilded Decorated with gold.

gold leaf An extremely thin layer of gold.

henna A reddish dye made from the powdered leaves of the henna plant that grows in Asia and North Africa.

Ice Age A period of time when large parts of the earth were covered with ice. The last Ice Age lasted from around 100,000 years ago to 10,000 years ago.

jackal mask A mask made to look like a wild desert dog called a jackal. The jackal was the symbol of the Egyptian god Anubis.

jade A semiprecious stone that can range in color from green to white.

lapis lazuli A bright turquoise-blue mineral found in rocks.

lichen A flat, moss-like plant that grows on trees and rocks.

loincloth A piece of cloth worn around the waist or hips and covering the bottom.

mica A type of rock that can be split into very thin sheets.

moccasin A shoe made from soft leather.

motif A figure or shape in a design.

mural A wall painting.

nomad A member of a tribe or people that wander from place to place.

obsidian A dark, glassy, volcanic rock.

ocher A type of rock or earth that is used for making brown, red, orange, and yellow pigments.

pectoral A large ornament worn on the chest.

pigment A natural substance, such as a plant or a rock, that gives color to something.

plaid A design of straight lines crossing at right angles to give a checkered appearance.

plaque A small, flat brooch or badge.

pleated Folded and pressed or stitched in place.

quartz A gemstone that can be purple, brown, yellow, or pink in color.

rouge Red powder or paste applied to the cheeks.

saffron An orange-yellow color, usually made from crocus flowers.

sandalwood A sweet-smelling wood.

sardonyx A gemstone with reddish-brown and white stripes.

sarong A draped, skirtlike garment made from a strip of cloth.

scabbard A holder for a sword or dagger.

scalloped Wavy, or made up of a series of curves.

sediment Solid bits that settle at the bottom of a liquid.

serpentine A dark green rock with a shiny surface.

standard-bearer Someone who carries the flag (or standard) for a company of soldiers.

tasseled Decorated with bunches of threads that are tied at one end.

tepee A conical tent made by Native Americans.

terracotta A type of hard, unglazed pottery that is brownish-red in color.

tiered Having several layers.

tuber A kind of plant root.

wicker A flexible twig or shoot, often used for weaving.

Adult General Reference Sources

Fagan, Brian M., *Kingdoms of Gold, Kingdoms of Jade: The Americas before Columbus* (Thames and Hudson, 1991)

Sichel, Marion, *Costume of the Classical World* (Batsford, 1980)

Starr, Chester G., *A History of the Ancient World* (Oxford, 1991)

Symons, David, *Costume of Ancient Greece* (Batsford, 1987)

Symons, David, *Costume of Ancient Rome* (Batsford, 1987)

Watson, Philip, *Costume of Ancient Egypt* (Chelsea House, 1987)

Wise, Terence, *Ancient Armies of the Middle East* (Osprey, 1981)

Young Adult Sources

Chandler, Fiona, *The Ancient World* (Usborne, 1999)

Chisholm, Jane, *The Usborne Book of the Ancient World* (Usborne, 1991)

Cotterell, Arthur, *The Encyclopedia of Ancient Civilizations* (Mayfield, 1983)

Haywood, John (Ed), *Everyday Life in the Ancient World: The Illustrated History Encyclopedia* (Southwater, 2001)

Millard, Anne, *The Atlas of the Ancient World* (Dorling Kindersley, 1994)

Internet Resources

http://www.costumes.org/history/100pages/greeklinks.htm

A general website on the history of costume with links to sites on different cultures of the ancient world and their costumes.

http://www.costumes.org

The Costumer's Manifesto A general website on the history of costume with links to sites on different cultures, and their costumes.

http://www.smith.edu/hsc/museum/ancient_ inventions/home.htm
The Smith College Museum of Ancient Inventions has recreations of prehistoric and ancient textile tools with descriptions of their uses.

http://www.digitalegypt.ucl.ac.uk
Digital Egypt for Universities includes multiple pages on textile production; tools and clothing in ancient Egypt, including many color photos and pattern diagrams of surviving garments; also images of jewelry and tools for body art.

http://www.reshafim.org.il/ad/egypt/timelines /topics/clothing.htm
Ancient Egypt: Clothing page with diagrams, photos, and detailed bibliography and links.

http://www.davidclaudon.com/Cleo/ Cleopatra1.html
The Cleopatra Costume on Stage and in Film examines in detail both the probable clothing of the real Cleopatra, as well as the theatrical costumes worn by performers depicting her since the sixteenth century.

http://phoenicia.org/dress.html
Phoenician Dress, Ornaments and Social Habits: an outline of ancient Phoenician dress of all classes, with footnotes.

http://www.annaswebart.com/culture/ costhistory/
Greek Costume through the Centuries concentrates mainly on women's dress from the Minoan Civilization to the nineteenth century.

http://www.greyhawkes.com/blacksword/ Spartan%20Combat%20Arts%202001/ 1-Pages/HowTo/Clothing/Chiton.htm
How to Make a Chiton: instructions for making ancient Greek female dress.

http://www.add.gr/jewel/elka/index.html
Greek Jewelry: Five Thousand Years of Tradition has beautiful photographs, and a detailed history of the subject.

http://www.villaivilla.com/
Villa Ivilla, where you can "become acquainted with the rhythm of daily life in ancient Rome and learn about fashions for men and women, dining and cuisine, and home life." The site includes instructions for correctly wrapping a toga.

http://www.vroma.org/~bmcmanus/ romanpages.html
Rome: Republic to Empire has a section on Roman clothing with many details of accessories for both men and women, including diagrams for recreating them.

http://www.roman-empire.net/society/ soc-dress.html
Roman Dress, part of the Illustrated History of the Roman Empire site, has photos, diagrams, and detailed information on Roman clothing styles.

http://www.library.utoronto.ca/east/students 03/tai_amy/
The Evolution of Chinese Costume covers changes in Chinese dress from ancient times to the present.

Index